Editor
Kim Fields

Managing Editor
Ina Massler Levin, M.A.

Illustrator
Vicki Frazier

Cover Artist
Marilyn Goldberg

Art Production Manager
Kevin Barnes

Imaging
Rosa C. See

Publisher
Mary D. Smith, M.S. Ed.

Mysteries for Writing and Critical Thinking

It was a dark and stormy night...

Author

Leif Hanson

Teacher Created Resources, Inc.
6421 Industry Way
Westminster, CA 92683
www.teachercreated.com

ISBN: 978-1-4206-3026-8

©2006 Teacher Created Resources, Inc.
Reprinted, 2013
Made in U.S.A.

Table of Contents

Introduction

The objective of Mysteries for Writing and Critical Thinking is to provide students, fifth grade and above, with higher-level thinking activities and writing prompts. Each mystery requires the students to break down the clues, filter through the evidence, and form an opinion of the guilty party. The clues call on the class to use everything from deductive reasoning to math and science skills. The teacher can have the class discuss the evidence after the students have had the chance to look at the clues. In this way, students who are having trouble getting started can get needed help. Each mystery also serves as a writing prompt. There are actually enough facts in each case to say any of the characters are guilty. A student can construct a persuasive paper pretending to be an attorney. The focus would be on the strength of the argument and the use of the evidence. The student can also step into the shoes of one of the suspects and write a narrative. Or the student could pretend to be an investigator and write an expository paper explaining the major clues in the case.

For a culminating activity, hold a court case or a run-through of the evidence, providing the students with a second opportunity to look at the case in a new way and allowing them to re-form opinions.

Possible discussion prompts are included for each mystery. The teacher can determine how much to give away (if modifications are needed). The prompts are only some of the possible questions to ask. The students will come up with theories that are not included; as long as the answers make sense, they are correct. After one or two of the mysteries, the class should be able to carry out a discussion on its own.

To help with the discussion, the teacher should work through a mystery prior to presenting it to the class. The teacher should try to prove each suspect's guilt while doing this. This should help ease the element of surprise when discussing each mystery with the class.

After the teacher has worked through the mysteries, he or she should look at the answer key (pages 74–80) to get the correct answers. Most importantly, the emphasis should always be placed on a well-supported argument. As long as an argument makes sense, it should be considered correct. Emphasize to students that in the United States a suspect is presumed innocent until there is enough evidence to prove him or her guilty. However, the students need to understand that sometimes innocent people go to jail and guilty people are set free.

Before beginning a mystery, review with students the concept of a "red herring." Tell the students that in a mystery, the author often presents irrelevant information to distract the reader's attention away from the original problem. In other words, these unnecessary tidbits try to throw the reader off the trail of the correct solution. Emphasize to the students that they will need to separate the valid evidence from the red herrings.

Writing Lesson Outline

Day One

1. Provide a copy of a mystery for each student.

2. Read the mystery as a class.

3. Allow the students to work in small groups to review the material and gather clues.

4. Have the class discuss possible clues.

5. Assign detective work (gathering clues) for homework.

Day Two

1. Students break up into the different suspect groups as they discuss the clues.

2. Allow the students to switch groups as they change their minds.

3. Assign introduction of paper for homework: topic sentence and three reasons.

Day Three

1. Discuss any other possible clues.

2. Students share introductions and peer-edit. Make sure the three reasons do not overlap.

3. Assign first draft for homework.

Day Four

1. Peer-edit papers and conference with students.

2. Students prepare for court.

3. Assign final draft for homework.

Day Five

1. Collect final drafts.

2. Take a class vote to see how many think each suspect is guilty. Leave numbers on the board.

3. Volunteers can become prosecutors and defenders and present their cases to the class.

4. The rest of the class is the jury. They will deliberate and determine a verdict. For an added challenge, the jury cannot convict a suspect unless the verdict is unanimous—otherwise, majority rules.

5. Go over all of the evidence as a class. Review any evidence that might have been missed. Reveal the answer for each mystery (pages 74–80).

Additional Activities

Writing Prompts

To convict or defend a suspect requires a great deal of evidence, so the end product of these prompts will be paragraphs with a great deal of support. A student could also step into the shoes of one of the suspects and write a narrative, explaining his or her side of the story.

Debate Topics

For these activities, the focus is to construct intelligent, supported arguments. The debate could take place in a "jury room" and could be easily turned into a game. Slip a note to a few students asking them to defend a certain suspect. A student gets points for each jury member that takes his or her side. See which student ends up with the most points.

Classroom Center

With many clues to digest and ponder, students will stay busy trying to solve the mysteries at a center.

Student Challenges

After solving the mysteries, challenge students to defend the guilty party or convict another suspect.

Cross-Curricular Knowledge

Some of the cases require students to draw on their science and mathematical backgrounds. Encourage students to research careers that use this type of "detective" knowledge to find solutions at work. Here are some examples:

➡ crime-scene investigator　　➡ lab researcher　　➡ engineer

Critical-Thinking Exercises

Students will begin to make logical arguments and think of all possible sides before reaching a conclusion. Have students read several transcripts from actual court cases that interest them. Instruct the students to study the words of the prosecution and the defense, along with the jury's decision.

Script Writing

Students can take the facts of the case and then elaborate on them to develop a play. Each case could be turned into a mock trial. After the "lawyers" present their cases, the class could vote on the verdict.

Art Project

After hearing the facts, students can draw a comic strip to show what they think really happened. The teacher could pair up students, with one student acting as a witness and the other as a police sketch artist. The witness uses detailed vocabulary and adjectives to describe a suspect while the artist sketches a face to match the description. The class could then guess which suspect the drawing most resembles.

Write Your Own Mystery

After solving a few of the puzzles in the book, try to construct a mystery of your own. Follow the outline below to create an original mystery. Provide at least three suspects, and see if your classmates can use the clues you provide to find the guilty party.

The Victim(s):

Date and Time of the Crime:

The Crime Scene:

Summary of the Crime:

The Suspects:

Witnesses to the Crime:

Mystery #1

DELIVERY OR TAKE-OUT?

NOTE: All people in this story are fictional. (I bet you could have figured that out, though!)

Background Information

The authorities received a call from Mr. Les Cash one evening about a break-in that occurred in his apartment. When the officers arrived at the scene, Mr. Cash told them that he was missing $10,000. The officers then took photographs and dusted for fingerprints. It was not long before they brought Dee Liver in for questioning.

Witnesses

"Yes, that's him."

➡ *statement made by an 80-year-old man who picked the accused out of a lineup*

"I saw him leaving the apartment one night with money in his hand."

➡ *statement made by a female physician*

DELIVERY OR TAKE—OUT?

The Accused

Dee Liver has been arrested before for shoplifting. He lives in the neighborhood and delivers pizzas for a living. He has delivered to the victim's apartment before. His monthly income is $600. His brother is a locksmith. At his residence a credit card bill was found. He owed $2,500, which was due in a week. Two weeks after the crime, he purchased a new computer system.

DELIVERY OR TAKE—OUT?

The Victim

Les Cash reported having over $10,000 in cash stolen from his apartment. Bank statements show that this amount was withdrawn from his account.

The Crime Scene

➥ Muddy footprints (the same size and brand as Dee's shoes) were found in the apartment.

➥ Fingerprints of the accused were also discovered inside the apartment. Only the bedroom was a mess, which is where the money was reportedly kept. The front door and the windows were all locked. None of them were broken.

Questions About the Case

Set I

1. Based on the comments of the first witness, how would you explain why he chose Dee from a lineup? _____

_____

_____

2. Do you think lineups are accurate? Why or why not?

_____

_____

_____

3. What features of the first witness could make him an unreliable witness? _____

_____

4. How could Dee's occupation be related to the account of the second witness? _____

_____

_____

5. The second witness wears eyeglasses. Does this automatically discredit her as a witness? Why or why not? _____

_____

_____

- -

Fold the following section under before copying this page for students.

Answers to Discussion Prompts (Set I)

1. The witness has probably seen Dee before. Dee might be guilty of the crime or he might resemble the person who really stole the money. **2.** Some estimates say that errors in criminal lineups range from 4% to 35%, depending on the type of crime. Some studies have shown that lineups are rigged against the innocent: if the real culprit is not in the lineup, then an innocent person will be chosen as the suspect. **3.** He wears eyeglasses. **4.** She saw him leaving the apartment, but Dee could have been delivering pizza. **5.** Even though she wears eyeglasses, she probably has good eyesight because physicians need to be able to see well to do their work. And, while eyeglasses are usually worn by people who can't see well on their own, they can be worn as a fashion statement by those who don't need them to see better.

DELIVERY OR TAKE – OUT?

Questions About the Case

Set II

1. What are some possible motives for Dee to steal the money?

   _____

   _____

   _____

   _____

2. What additional evidence would be helpful to determine if Dee is guilty? _____

   _____

   _____

   _____

3. What alternative methods could Dee use to fund his computer purchase if it costs more than he earns? _____

   _____

   _____

   _____

   _____

- -

Fold the following section under before copying this page for students.

Answers to Discussion Prompts (Set II)

1. He has stolen before and might have a bad habit. He owes more than he makes. **2.** What and when did he steal? Where did he steal from? Where does his brother live? What is their relationship like? **3.** He could have saved the money. He might be able to use his credit card to purchase the computer.

Questions About the Case

Set III

1. What can you conclude about the victim? _____

_____

_____

_____

_____

2. What can you infer about the apartment? _____

_____

_____

_____

_____

3. What is the connection between Dee's fingerprints being in the apartment and the crime? _____

_____

_____

_____

_____

- -

Fold the following section under before copying this page for students.

Answers to Discussion Prompts (Set III)

1. He says he had $10,000 dollars stolen. He did withdraw the money from his account. We don't know what he did with the money after he withdrew it from the bank. **2.** The living room is neat and not messed up. Only the bedroom is a mess. The robber would have to have known where the money was. Dee's footprints and fingerprints are in the apartment. It seems that the person did not break into the apartment because nothing is broken. **3.** He could have gone inside when he was delivering pizza; it never says where the fingerprints were found.

     #3026 Mysteries for Writing and Critical Thinking

(sidebar: DELIVERY OR TAKE—OUT?)

Mystery #2

THE CANINE CAPER

NOTE: All people in this story are fictional. (I bet you could have figured that out, though!)

The Victims

Karen and Scott S. Terrier

Karen and Scott S. Terrier raise prize-winning dogs for a living. They have had quite a canine career. Despite their love and gentle care, there have been several occasions where their hounds have escaped. Whether it is due to luck or the hefty reward they offer, their little award-winners are always returned safely. In fact, the Terriers thought their precious Snowball had made a break for it again.

They posted missing notices all over town. (See below for a copy of the poster.) They placed these notices in the same locations as usual since they have had good results all of the other times their dogs have been missing. A week later, instead of good news, the Terriers received a ransom note. After some investigating by the police, unidentified footprints were discovered at the scene of the crime.

Missing!

$5,000 Reward

Snowball

Date missing: 12/21/2003

Please contact:

  Karen and Scott S. Terrier

  1234 Kennel Drive

  555-1234

THE CANINE CAPER

The Ransom Note

THE CANINE CAPER

The Crime Scene

These footprints were found at the crime scene.

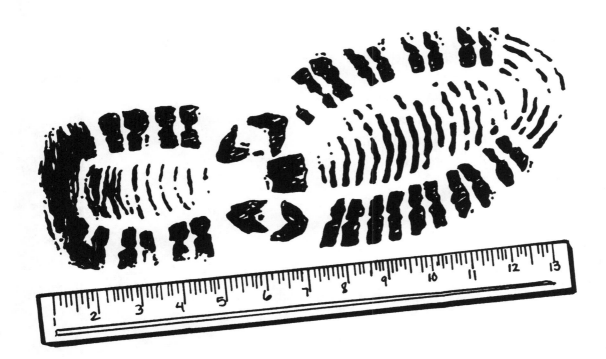

THE CANINE CAPER

The Suspects

Herman Shepherd

Mr. Shepherd has several ties to the victims. Besides being the owner of the dog who finished second to Snowball at the last dog show, he also purchased a puppy from the Terriers the day before Snowball disappeared. He went to the Terriers' residence to pick the pooch up.

The old saying of "dog is a man's best friend" definitely holds true in Mr. Shepherd's case. In fact, his dogs seem to be his only friends. He cares about only two things: his prized pets and winning. He has been known to stop at nothing to see his pooches parading on the winner's podium. He was caught at one show possessing a jar of fleas; coincidentally enough, he had not brought his dog in yet!

A witness heard Mr. Shepherd making threats directed at the perennial champion, Snowball, the day after he and his pooch had lost another competition to that bundle of blinding white fur. He denies making any threats. He is a wealthy man, but even his money cannot dethrone the queen of canines, Snowball. (***See Exhibit A on page 19.***)

Alice Cannuski

Miss Cannuski is the next-door neighbor of the Terriers. To say that she is not an animal lover would be an understatement. She has made several calls to the authorities with false claims of late-night noise coming from the Terriers' kennels. She has written several harassing notes to the Terriers. (***See Exhibit B on page 20.***)

Amy, Rick, and Pete Bull

The Bulls returned Snowball the last time she ran away. They used to own a pet store but had to sell it shortly after Pete's birth because of his violent reactions to animal fur. The Bulls own the restaurant where Mr. Shepherd supposedly made the threats directed at Snowball. Mr. Bull is the witness who heard Mr. Shepherd. (***See Exhibit C on page 20.***)

THE CANINE CAPER

Exhibit A

These are the directions that Mr. Shepherd evidently used to pick up his puppy from the Terriers. This was found hanging on a wall near where Mr. Shepherd keeps his dogs.

Dog Kennel

garage (dogs sleep)

1234

1232

Neighbor

Take route 80 to Exit A. Left at light. Right on Kennel Drive (1234).

(12/20 1:30)

Exhibit B

This is Miss Cannuski's latest note to the Terriers. They thought it would be a good idea to save it in case she called the authorities again so that they could show the police how unreasonable she has become.

> Mr. and Mrs. Terrier,
>
> I have been nice up to this point, but my patience is wearing thin. The noise your dogs make is unbearable. I have tried to talk to you on several occassions, but I feel you are not taking my complaints seriously. Consider this my final attempt at being neighborly.
>
> A. Cannuski

Exhibit C

Worried that the police might accuse them, the Bulls offered this prescription bottle to support their claim of Pete's allergies to animal fur, which were confirmed by their family physician. They also handed over real-estate contracts supporting their story of the thriving pet store business that they were forced to sell.

Rx

Pete Bull

1 capsule every
4 hours, if needed.

Filled: 12/22/03

Expires: 1/22/04

Questions About the Case

Set I

1. What generalizations can be made about the Terriers? _____

_____

_____

_____

2. What information from the poster is important to use when solving the mystery? _____

_____

_____

_____

_____

3. After analyzing the facts in this case, what leads you to believe that the Terriers have money? _____

_____

_____

_____

_____

- -

Fold the following section under before copying this page for students.

Answers to Discussion Prompts (Set I)

1. They raise dogs. Their dogs run away often. In the past, they have always found their dogs. **2.** Snowball went missing on 12/21/2003. The reward is $5,000. **3.** They have offered $5,000 for the return of their dog. The couple thought that Snowball ran away again, which would mean they most likely have offered this reward on numerous occasions.

THE CANINE CAPER

Questions About the Case

Set II

1. What is the function of a ransom note composed entirely from cutout letters? _____

_____

_____

_____

2. What details would you select from the ransom note to show that its author knows the Terriers well? _____

_____

_____

_____

3. What is the relationship between each suspect and the revealed information in the ransom note? _____

_____

_____

_____

_____

Fold the following section under before copying this page for students.

Answers to Discussion Prompts (Set II)

1. The culprit wishes to remain anonymous by disguising his or her handwriting. **2.** You might select the dog's name and the bank that the Terriers use. **3.** Alice is the neighbor, so she might know a lot about the Terriers. Herman shows dogs at many of the same competitions as the Terriers. The Bulls have returned Snowball to the Terriers before. The Terriers might have paid with a check at the restaurant.

THE CANINE CAPER

Questions About the Case

Set III

1. What judgment can you make about the footprints? _____

   _____

   _____

   _____

2. Can you formulate a theory for the condition of the treads in the footprints? _____

   _____

   _____

   _____

3. How is the size of the shoe related to the person to whom it belongs?

   _____

   _____

   _____

   _____

- -

Fold the following section under before copying this page for students.

Answers to Discussion Prompts (Set III)

1. Running shoes would leave this type of print; they have a certain shape and type of tread. **2.** Some of the treads are worn out, so the person might exercise or the shoes might be old. **3.** A shoe size can tell the approximate height of a person (for example, if a shoe is small, it probably doesn't belong to a tall person).

THE CANINE CAPER

Questions About the Case

Set IV

1. What are possible motives for Herman? _____

_____

_____

_____

_____

2. What are possible motives for Alice? _____

_____

_____

_____

_____

3. What are possible motives for the Bulls? _____

_____

_____

_____

_____

- -

Fold the following section under before copying this page for students.

Answers to Discussion Prompts (Set IV)

1. He hates to lose. He supposedly made threats. He has been to the Terriers' residence before. **2.** She hates dogs. She has made threats. **3.** They have returned Snowball before and might need the money.

THE CANINE CAPER

Questions About the Case

Set V

1. How can you use Herman's notes to speculate that he is guilty of the crime? _____

   _____

   _____

   _____

   _____

   _____

2. Elaborate on the possible legitimate reasons Herman would take detailed notes about the Terriers' dogs. _____

   _____

   _____

   _____

   _____

   _____

- -

Fold the following section under before copying this page for students.

Answers to Discussion Prompts (Set V)

1. He noted where the dogs sleep and the location of the kennel. He was at the house the day before the disappearance of Snowball. **2.** He always loses to the Terriers, so maybe he wants to raise his dogs in a similar fashion. He might want to make sure that he doesn't get lost when picking up his new puppy.

Questions About the Case

Set VI

1. How can you use Alice's note to speculate that she is guilty of the crime?

_____

_____

_____

_____

_____

2. What evidence provided by the Bulls justifies being suspicious of them?

_____

_____

_____

_____

_____

- -

Fold the following section under before copying this page for students.

Answers to Discussion Prompts (Set VI)

1. She seems very angry and makes threats. On the other hand, she hates animals, so why would she want to steal a dog? **2.** Pete's prescription was filled the day after Snowball disappeared. If Pete has such violent reactions, his parents would not let him near animals. However, if the Bulls took Snowball, Pete would need to take medicine to treat his dog-fur allergies. Rick Bull says he heard Mr. Shepherd make threats at the restaurant, but no one else can support this claim.

THE CANINE CAPER

Mystery #3

A "LOTTO" LIES

NOTE: All people in this story are fictional. (I bet you could have figured that out, though!)

Background Information

On August 25, 2004, the police received a call from Will Winmoney claiming that his co-worker, Ivan Cash, had purchased a lottery ticket for him the day before, and failed to return it to him. The drawing time for this lottery was at 12:00 p.m. The ticket contained the winning numbers and was worth $20 million. The contest officials have been notified of the situation, and no prize money will be awarded until the authorities can come to a proper conclusion. If a clear case cannot be presented for either person, the money will be held over for next week's drawing.

The Winning Ticket

A "Lotto" Money to be Won

2   4   11   18   29   31
6   7   12   19   22   24
3   9   13   16   21   25

Numbers to be drawn at
12:00 noon
Date: 8/23/05
Time purchased: 11:30 a.m.

A "LOTTO" LIES

Will Winmoney's Statement

A "LOTTO" LIES

"It was lunch time, and Ivan stopped by my office and said he was going out to the market on his lunch break to pick up some lunch and a few groceries because he and his wife were having company for dinner at 7:00 P.M. He asked if I needed anything, so I gave him a $5 bill and a list—which of course he cannot find. On it, I asked him to pick up a dozen apples and a lottery ticket. I asked him to get a $3 lottery ticket. Each line of numbers costs a dollar, and I thought I would let the computer generate two of the lines; but the first line is the same set of numbers I always play. They are my daughters' birthdays. My first daughter, April, was born just before May. My second daughter, Autumn, was born in November. My last daughter, Winter, was born in February. There is no coincidence here: those are my daughters' birthdays, and that is my winning ticket.

"I thought Ivan might be a little jealous when I received that promotion and raise, but this is crazy. I do not know if this is revenge for denting his car in the parking lot or for giving him a poor evaluation. How can he sit there and deny that this is my ticket? If I would have known this was going to happen, I would have gone to the store myself."

Ivan Cash's Statement

A "LOTTO" LIES

"I do this guy a favor and now he tries to take my money! I went to the market that day and picked up Will's apples. I asked the clerk for the winning numbers, and he wrote them down for me. I pulled out my ticket and could not believe it! I raced back to the office and decided to tell everyone at the end of the day that I would no longer be working there because of my lucky ticket.

"I gave Will his apples. He noticed that there were only 10 in the bag, so I had to go back to my car, open the dented door, and search for two pieces of fruit. I was mad. When I returned, he noticed that I still owed him a nickel or something ridiculous like that for change. I thought he was kidding, but the look on his face lacked any bit of humor. He might think I am mad at him for other things, and he would be right; but I am an honest guy. If it was his ticket, I would give it to him."

The Scene

This is the store where Ivan went shopping. The store clerk remembered seeing Ivan but could not recall the date the items were purchased.

Questions About the Case

Set I

1. How would you prioritize the evidence given in the information? What clues are the most important? _____

    _____

    _____

    _____

    _____

2. What evidence can you gather by studying the winning ticket? _____

    _____

    _____

    _____

    _____

Fold the following section under before copying this page for students.

Answers to Discussion Prompts (Set I)

1. The date and time stamped on the winning ticket give us needed information to solve the mystery. Will's claim is also an important clue.
2. The winning numbers and the time and date stamped on the ticket are all evidence in this case.

A "LOTTO" LIES

Questions About the Case

Set II

1. What evidence can you compile from Will's statement? _____

   _____

   _____

   _____

   _____

   _____

2. How could you test the validity of Will's statement? _____

   _____

   _____

   _____

   _____

   _____

   _____

Fold the following section under before copying this page for students.

Answers to Discussion Prompts (Set II)

1. He says the first line of the winning ticket corresponds with his daughters' birthdays. He gave Ivan $5, but he wanted a dozen apples and a $3 lottery ticket. He said that he dented Ivan's car and gave him a poor evaluation. He mentions that he received a promotion and a raise. **2.** Look carefully at the numbers on the winning ticket and compare them with his daughters' birthdays. Determine how much the apples really cost. Would $5 be enough to purchase a dozen apples and a lottery ticket?

A "LOTTO" LIES

Questions About the Case

Set III

1. What evidence can you compile from Ivan's statement?_____

_____

_____

_____

_____

_____

2. How could you test the validity of Ivan's statement? _____

_____

_____

_____

_____

_____

- -

Fold the following section under before copying this page for students.

Answers to Discussion Prompts (Set III)

1. He only mentions getting Will's apples. He says that Will noticed two missing apples and so he returned to his car. Will then noticed Ivan owed him a small amount of change. If Will is so careful to check his items and change, why did he not remember to get the ticket from Ivan? **2.** To test the validity of Ivan's statement, check the date on the winning ticket. Is it the date on which Will asked Ivan to buy apples?

A "LOTTO" LIES

Questions About the Case

Set IV

1. How could you explain the difference in the cost of apples by comparing Ivan's statement and the store sign? _____

_____

_____

_____

2. How can studying the scene result in possible clues to solve the mystery?

_____

_____

_____

_____

_____

_____

Fold the following section under before copying this page for students.

Answers to Discussion Prompts (Set IV)

1. The price for the apples could have been raised if they were on sale the day before. **2.** The store opens at noon. Therefore, the ticket could not have been purchased at this store on the date that Will claims. At $0.37 each, a dozen apples would cost $4.44. Students might conclude that Will is lying, but if they look back at Ivan's statement, he does mention giving change back to Will. Or, the price of apples could have changed.

A "LOTTO" LIES

Mystery #4

THE PUPIL WITH PEEKING PUPILS

NOTE: All people in this story are fictional. (I bet you could have figured that out, though!)

Background Information

Paige Turner

Stu Dent

Mr. Ed Ucate teaches 6th graders in St. Paul, Minnesota. His students had just returned from their winter vacations, and he thought it might be a good time to surprise them with a writing quiz. Mr. Ucate assigned the class a narrative paper with the subject of what had happened during the winter break. Although the class had just recently returned, the teacher thought this would be a nice opportunity for each student to raise his or her grade.

The only student Mr. Ucate was worried about was Paige Turner. Her family had moved from Australia over the break. sThe teacher was unsure of her writing abilities, but he thought it would be a good chance to get to know her writing style. He had not planned on grading her paper unless she did well.

Before giving the quiz, Mr. Ucate decided to change the seating chart. He put Paige at a desk to the left of one of his prized pupils, Stu Dent. Stu was an honor-roll student who always did well on quizzes and tests. Also, Stu and Paige were the only two left-handers in the class, and Mr. Ucate thought it might be nice for Paige to feel like she didn't stand out in that way. He knew that Stu liked his old seat next to his buddy (fellow straight-A student, Reid Abook), but Mr. Ucate felt that it would be good to change the classroom around a bit. Because most teachers at the school seated their students in alphabetical order, it seemed that Reid and Stu had been sitting next to each other for years.

As the writing quiz started, Mr. Ucate was called and had to leave the classroom. He returned shortly before the class was dismissed. The bell rang and the students stood up, formed a single-file line, and deposited their drafts on Mr. Ucate's desk.

Mr. Ucate brought the papers home and soon discovered a dilemma: two of the papers were almost identical, as if they were born just minutes apart. The two in question belonged to Stu and Paige. The teacher pondered, but he could not remember any obvious clues as to who cheated. However, after careful consideration of the classroom conditions and close observation of the papers, Mr. Ucate was able to conclude which pupil had peeking pupils.

Paige's Report

Here is a copy of the report Paige Turner submitted to Mr. Ucate.

Paige Turner
January 8, 2004
Writing

Did you What did you do on vacation? I had a great time, especially on December 28, 2003. I can't will never forget that day. It was the day of the neighborhood football championship.

It was the last quarter and the score was tied. My legs were sea cement and my heart was bouncing like a trampoline. I knew I could no longer play it so safe. I needed take a chance at scoring the winning goal. All of a sudden, Casey stole the ball from other team and kicked it my way. I so could see the ball fly soaring at me. I felt like I was in a movie that was being filmed in slow motion. The black and white act hexagons hovered in a hypnotizing pattern. I almost caught it, but my hands knew better than to touch the ball. The last thing my team needed was another penalty.

I sto trapped the ball like a hunter captures a beast and I started down the field. I was running so fo rapidly my red shorts seemed like the tail of a comet. I faked a pass and the defender bought it. He fell to the ground. I spun around and continued my marathon down the field. Nothing was going to stop me now. I was trying to catch my breath, but it seemed that it was the only thing that was faster than me. My feet were dribbling better than a newborn baby. I The goal was in sight.

As I sped past the last defender, the goalie's eyes and mine met. It was like we were in an old western movie and there was going to be a showdown. Their goalkeeper was a brick wall. I kept thinking about all the numerous shots that this fortress had blocked before. I no juked left and then to the right. The goalie bit my bait. He was a hungry fish. As he ran right I kicked the grass-stained sphere. My leg was a cannon. The ball whistled through the air and made a snapping sound when it hit the back of the net. My heart beat with the sound of the crowd. I collapsed to the ground and soon was at the bottom of a pile of teammates. I did it. I won the game.

Thinking back about that day, I remember the feeling of joy my heart felt. I had never really felt that before. I was usually the last one picked for teams—that is until my goal. I knew football is a team sports, but that was my goal. It gave me more than just the pride of winning the game. It gave me the confidence to believe in myself, which is much more valuable than any trophy. December 28, 2003, is one of the best days in my life!

Stu's Report

Here is a copy of the report Paige Turner submitted to Mr. Ucate.

Stu Dent

January 8, 2004

Writing

What did you do on vacation? I had a great time, especially on December 28, 2003. I will never forget that day. It was the day of the neighborhood football championship.

It was the last quarter and the score was tied. My legs were cement and my heart was bouncing like a trampoline. I knew I could no longer play it safe. I needed to take a chance at scoring the winning goal. All of a sudden, Casey stole the ball from the other team and kicked it my way. I could see the ball soaring at me. I felt like I was in a movie that was being filmed in slow motion. The black and white hexagons hovered in a hypnotizing pattern. I almost caught it, but my hands knew better than to touch the ball. The last thing my team needed was another penalty.

I trapped the ball like a hunter captures a beast and I started down the field. I was running so rapidly my red shorts seemed like the tail of a comet. I faked a pass and the defender bought it. He fell to the ground. I spun around and continued my marathon down the field. Nothing was going to stop me now. I was trying to catch my breath, but it seemed that it was the only thing that was faster than me. My feet were dribbling better than a newborn baby. The goal was in sight.

As I sped past the last defender, the goalie's eyes and mine met. It was like we were in an old western movie and there was going to be a showdown. Their goalkeeper was a brick wall. I kept thinking about the numerous shots that this fortress had blocked before. I juked left and then to the right. The goalie bit my bait. He was a hungry fish. As he ran right, I kicked the grass-stained sphere. My leg was a cannon. The ball whistled through the air and made a snapping sound when it hit the back of the net. My heart beat with the sound of the crowd. I collapsed to the ground and soon was at the bottom of a pile of teammates. I did it. I won the game.

Thinking back about that day, I remember the feeling of joy my heart felt. I had never really felt that before. I was usually the last one picked for teams—that is until my goal. I know football is a team sport, but that was my goal. It gave me more than just the pride of winning the game. It gave me the confidence to believe in myself, which is more valuable than any trophy. December 28, 2003 is one of the best days of my life!

Questions About the Case

Set I

1. Based on what you know about the assignment and the students involved, how would you explain the identical nature of the two papers?

   _____

   _____

   _____

   _____

   _____

2. As the teacher, how could you determine if a student copied a writing assignment? _____

   _____

   _____

   _____

   _____

Fold the following section under before copying this page for students.

Answers to Discussion Prompts (Set I)

1. One student copied another student's work. Both students could have been involved in the same event. **2.** Determine which paper has the least errors. Because this is a first draft, there should be crossed out words and some grammatical errors.

THE PUPIL WITH PEEKING PUPILS

Questions About the Case

Set II

1. What conclusions can you draw from examining Paige's paper?

_____

_____

_____

_____

_____

2. Do you think Paige cheated? Why or why not? _____

_____

_____

_____

_____

_____

- -

Fold the following section under before copying this page for students.

Answers to Discussion Prompts (Set II)

1. There are mistakes. She is playing soccer. She is wearing shorts in December, so the game had to take place in a warm climate. **2.** If *yes*: She is a new student from another country and is not used to the type of writing required in this class. She is seated by an honor-roll student, and she could have looked at his paper. If *no*: She has many mistakes, and a first draft would probably have these. She used to live in Australia, where it would be warm enough in December to wear shorts. Soccer is called football in Australia.

THE PUPIL WITH PEEKING PUPILS

Questions About the Case

Set III

1. What conclusions can you draw from examining Stu's paper?

_____

_____

_____

_____

_____

2. Do you think Stu cheated? Why or why not? _____

_____

_____

_____

_____

_____

Fold the following section under before copying this page for students.

Answers to Discussion Prompts (Set III)

1. Nothing is crossed out. There are no mistakes. **2.** If *no*: Stu is an honor-roll student and gets good grades. Stu is used to this type of assignment, since he's been in this teacher's class for several months. If *yes*: Stu's paper doesn't have any mistakes; most first drafts would have some mistakes. Stu would not use the word *football* to describe a soccer game he participated in.

THE PUPIL WITH PEEKING PUPILS

Mystery #5

RUNNING HOME WITH A HOME RUN

NOTE: All people in this story are fictional. (I bet you could have figured that out, though!)

Note to Teacher: Have each student color the stain green on Owen Aseat's baseball on page 44.

Background Information

The baseballs pictured below are more than mere souvenirs. One of them is a piece of history. The other is nothing more than a fake.

*Owen Aseat's
baseball*

*Jason A. Homer's
baseball*

The date was Sunday, August 10. The time was 8:30 p.m. Just three home runs were needed to cement Able Sworstenemy's place in history. Three more would give him a tie for the most career home runs. The press predicted Pittsburgh would be the site for the record, but Able Sworstenemy does not like to wait. Able stepped up to the plate in the seventh inning of the game and swung his way into the baseball record books. With one swing of his lethal lumber, he demolished the career home-run record. In the last game before the team headed to the Steel City, Able not only tied the record, he smashed it! He hit four home runs in his last game at home before his team went on a 10-game road trip.

The front office tried to locate the fan that caught the ball but had little luck. However, on Monday morning they received a call from Mr. Aseat claiming he had snagged the ball. Officials were ecstatic to have found the fan and the ball . . . until they received another call only 30 minutes later from Mr. Homer, claiming *he* had caught the ball.

RUNNING HOME WITH A HOME RUN

The Scene

The Star Dome, built in 1970, has been the setting for many historical happenings. Perhaps the greatest is the recently contested home-run baseball. Interestingly enough, most fans had purchased a ticket for the Pittsburgh series, the next set of games, due to the fact that most fans believed Able Sworstenemy would break the career home-run record there since he was just four shy of the feat. In the history of baseball, there have been very few players to hit four home runs in one game. Leave it to the King of Swing to prove people wrong!

The Evidence

Baseball officials reviewed video footage to see if any information could be gathered. Unfortunately, the only piece of evidence that could be salvaged was a shot of the mitt that was used to catch the ball. The person was shielded by a post in the outfield section of seats. The owners have received hundreds of complaints from paying customers about their obstructed view; ironically, the owners are the ones that are complaining about the view this time!

Here is a still image from the video footage of the mitt that caught Able's home run.

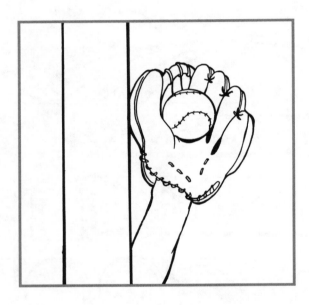

Jason A. Homer

Jason purchased a ticket to the game, never expecting to see history or catch a ball worth a million dollars. He claimed he purchased nachos at the game but failed to produce a receipt. The employee working behind the concession stand could not confirm or deny Jason's claim. Due to an auto accident, Mr. Homer had to sign his statement with his left hand. Witnesses also had to sign his statement, since the signature did not match his usual penmanship.

The Evidence (cont.)

Owen Aseat

Owen Aseat has been a season-ticket holder for the past 20 years. He usually uses his seats to persuade potential clients. He claims he called home on his cell phone after he caught the priceless piece of baseball lore. Authorities confirmed that he did indeed use his cell phone to call home. As further proof of his attendance, he also claims that the bottom part of his driver-side door was dented in the parking lot while he was at the game. He did not stop to complain to the attendant on duty, since he wanted to race home and share the news with his wife

The stadium's parking lot is usually filmed by surveillance cameras, but the attendant forgot to turn them on until right after the game. Mr. Aseat could not produce a parking receipt. The spot he said he parked at was filmed as being empty immediately after the game. His alleged spot was between the two large sports utility vehicles shown on this page.

*Parking Space Mr. Aseat Claims
To Have Been Parked In*

*Mr. Aseat's Car, Which He
Claims Was Dented at the Game*

Questions About the Case

Set I

1. What clues would you select from the Background Information to help solve this case? _____

_____

_____

_____

_____

_____

2. How could the office staff determine the rightful owner of the home-run baseball? _____

_____

_____

_____

_____

_____

_____

- -

Fold the following section under before copying this page for students.

Answers to Discussion Prompts (Set I)

1. One baseball is grass-stained; the other is not. Mr. Aseat and Mr. Homer are two possible owners of the home-run baseball. **2.** They could examine both baseballs closely.

RUNNING HOME WITH A HOME RUN

Questions About the Case

Set II

1. What conclusions can you draw from the information on Star Dome?

_____

_____

_____

_____

2. Why do you think fans would buy a ticket for the next game over a ticket for the game in question? _____

_____

_____

_____

_____

- -

Fold the following section under before copying this page for students.

Answers to Discussion Prompts (Set II)

1. It is an older structure. It is an indoor stadium and wouldn't have real grass. **2.** Since the press predicted the next series would be when Able would break the record, most people might have waited to attend a game then. Four home runs in one game is a rare feat.

RUNNING HOME WITH A HOME RUN

Questions About the Case

Set III

1. What evidence can you find in the video footage? _____

   _____

   _____

   _____

   _____

   _____

2. What evidence would you use to support the view that Jason caught the home run? _____

   _____

   _____

   _____

   _____

   _____

   _____

Fold the following section under before copying this page for students.

Answers to Discussion Prompts (Set III)

1. The person used his left hand to catch the ball, so the catcher of the ball would probably be right-handed. **2.** He did have a ticket to the game. He is right-handed, so he would wear a mitt on his left hand, as is shown in the video.

R U N N I N G   H O M E   W I T H   A   H O M E   R U N

Questions About the Case

Set IV

1. What inferences can you make from the two vehicles in the picture of the parking lot? _____

   _____

   _____

   _____

   _____

   _____

2. What evidence would you use to support the view that Owen caught the home-run hit? _____

   _____

   _____

   _____

   _____

   _____

   _____

Fold the following section under before copying this page for students.

Answers to Discussion Prompts (Set IV)

1. Owen's car is low to the ground. The sports utility vehicles are high above the ground. His car is damaged at the bottom; it's not likely that his car was dented during the game. **2.** He does have tickets for the entire season. He takes clients to the game. He says he used his cell phone to call home. He says his car was dented while he was at the game.

RUNNING HOME WITH A HOME RUN

Mystery #6

A PILEUP OF CARS AND PROBLEMS

> **NOTE:** All people in this story are fictional. (I bet you could have figured that out, though!)

Note to Teacher: Have each student color the color in the scratch on each license plate on page 55 as follows:

	Car A	Car B	Car C	Car D
Front Plate	leave blank	green mark	yellow mark	red mark
Back Plate	yellow mark	leave mark	green mark	green mark

Additionally, have the students color in each vehicle as follows:

page 56	page 57	page 58	page 59
white	green	red	yellow

Background Information

Time: Monday morning, 8:00 A.M. (The accident occurred at approximately 7:45 A.M.)

By the time the authorities arrived, the accident scene had been cleared by tow-truck drivers and street sweepers. Expecting to see the pile-up of four cars that was radioed in, the officer only spotted the four people involved in the accident. He contacted headquarters and was informed to investigate the automobiles at the lot after taking statements from the four individuals.

He knew that he needed to get the correct order of vehicles, since the person driving in the rear of the pile-up is usually to blame, especially in an accident that occurs at a stoplight. He also predicted that the people would not be too cooperative because they would not want to incriminate themselves.

The officer hoped to learn all he could from the people and the accident scene. He jotted down a diagram of the scene and then took the first person's statement.

Here is the officer's initial diagram of the accident:

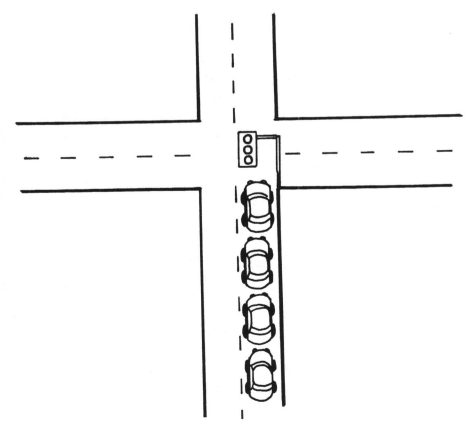

A PILE-UP OF CARS AND PROBLEMS

The Suspects

Dr. Otto Mobile

"I cannot believe this has happened. I have been driving for over 40 years and have never been involved in an accident. Someone's careless driving is going to make me late for my lecture at 11:00 A.M. I was even driving behind a woman who was dancing in her car, and I was *still* able to concentrate enough to not cause a wreck."

Ken Notstop

"What else can go wrong? First, I hear my team trades Able Sworstenemy, and then this. I was just heading over to a buddy's house, and this is what I get. All I know is I am not paying for any of this. I just retired last month from my tree business and I cannot afford to pay for someone else's mistake."

Kelly Sion

"Officer, I really need to go. How long do I have to stay here? I need to have the gym opened by noon or else we will get fined by the landlord. I always try to get there so I can exercise before the classes start. I've got that song stuck in my head. Do you mind if I go for a jog?"

Anita Newcar

"You need to talk to the person who has trees in his car. This is his fault. I do not think it is legal to be carrying loose birds around in a car. Now, I did not actually see birds, but if I were you I would check it out. There is a nest in one of those trees. Secondly, I am going to get written up for being late. I needed to be at work at 7:30 A.M. to process the overdue fines. Is the bird man going to get me a new job?"

A PILE-UP OF CARS AND PROBLEMS

The Scene

After speaking with all of the people involved, the officer collected phone numbers and the license plates that had apparently fallen off the cars. The officer brought these with him to the lot when he went to check the vehicles. Drivers are required to place vehicle stickers on the front plates.

KEYSTONE STATE
ICU83PL88
PENNSYLVANIA

KEYSTONE STATE
IH8MOOVV
PENNSYLVANIA

KEYSTONE STATE
ICU83PL88
PENNSYLVANIA

KEYSTONE STATE
IH8MOOVV
PENNSYLVANIA

KEYSTONE STATE
UUD2UUNX
PENNSYLVANIA

KEYSTONE STATE
NE14NSA
PENNSYLVANIA

KEYSTONE STATE
UUD2UUNX
PENNSYLVANIA

KEYSTONE STATE
NE14NSA
PENNSYLVANIA

A PILE-UP OF CARS AND PROBLEMS

The Evidence, Part I

The officer then went to the lot where all four of the vehicles had been towed. He hoped that by investigating the contents of each vehicle and using his notes, he could then match the plates to the cars and get a better understanding of what actually happened. The officer would take photos of each of the vehicles, exterior and interior, and go for test drives to see if any of the blame could be placed on poor maintenance.

When the officer turned on the first vehicle, he instinctively turned the station since the static was deafening. He knew this went against everything he had learned in the academy, but his reflexes had gotten the better of him. He just had to turn the knob back and forth a few times. This automobile passed with flying colors, with the exception of the horn. It was on the softer side, as far as car horns are concerned.

The Evidence, Part II

The second vehicle had a sports' talk program blasting on the radio. Once again the officer noted the station before he turned the radio off. The steering was a bit misaligned, and the brakes needed to be adjusted. Before he left, his curiosity grabbed hold of him like a seatbelt and pulled him to the backseat, where there was a bird's nest in one of the trees.

The Evidence, Part III

By the time he checked the third automobile, the officer had wondered if he was the only person that did not blast his radio early in the morning. Before he could turn down the rock anthem, it was over. The officer took the car for a short drive and discovered that the brakes had to have extreme pressure applied to them before the vehicle would come to a complete stop.

The Evidence, Part IV

The officer put the key into the ignition of the final vehicle with one hand and, preparing for the worst, moved his other hand to the volume knob. He was greeted by the soft, gentle words of the radio newscasters. Ironically, the officer had to turn up the radio in this vehicle, since the brakes complained and made a metallic grinding noise every time the brake pedal was pushed down.

In order for the officer to solve this case, he must figure out who owns which vehicle. Then he must figure out the order of the vehicles in relation to his initial diagram. Finally, he must strengthen his case by using the evidence to reveal how the guilty party caused the accident.

Questions About the Case

Set I

1. How could the officer prove who was at fault? _____

    _____

    _____

    _____

    _____

    _____

2. What clues are useful in the Background Information? _____

    _____

    _____

    _____

    _____

    _____

- -

Fold the following section under before copying this page for students.

Answers to Discussion Prompts (Set I)

1. If he determines the order of the vehicles, the car in back is usually to blame. **2.** The accident happened at 7:45 A.M. Four vehicles were involved in the accident. The accident happened at a stoplight.

A PILE-UP OF CARS AND PROBLEMS

Questions About the Case

Set II

1. What conclusions can you draw from Dr. Mobile's statement? _____

_____

_____

_____

2. What evidence can you compile from Ken's statement? _____

_____

_____

_____

3. What information can you learn from Kelly's statement? _____

_____

_____

_____

4. Which clues are important in Anita's statement? _____

_____

_____

_____

Fold the following section under before copying this page for students.

Answers to Discussion Prompts (Set II)

1. He said he was driving behind someone and saw a person dancing, so his car was not first in the pile-up. He has a lecture to give at 11:00 A.M., so he's probably not in a hurry. **2.** He was angry because a good player was traded. He was going to a friend's house. He used to have a tree business. **3.** She needs to open the gym by noon, so she's probably not in a hurry. However, she does go early to exercise. She has a song stuck in her head. **4.** She was driving behind someone, so her car was not first in the pile-up. She was driving behind a man who had a nest in his car. She is late for work and says she will be written up.

A PILE-UP OF CARS AND PROBLEMS

Questions About the Case

Set III

1. How could vanity plates help solve this case? _____

   _____

   _____

   _____

2. Who would you assign each set of plates to? Why? _____

   _____

   _____

   _____

   _____

   _____

3. How could the license plates be used as clues to find out who was at
   fault in this accident? _____

   _____

   _____

   _____

Fold the following section under before copying this page for students.

Answers to Discussion Prompts (Set III)

1. The decoded plates read: "I see you ate three plates," "I hate movies,"
"Used to use an axe," and "Anyone for an essay." A vanity plate usually tells
something about the driver of a car. **2.** Kelly—ICU83PL88 because she
works at a gym, Anita—IH8MOOVV because she is a librarian, Ken—
UUD2UUNX because he was a landscaper, and Otto—NE14NSA because he
is a teacher. **3.** It would depend on which plate has which color mark and if
it was the front or back plate. ICU83PL88 did not hit another car; therefore, it
was first in the lineup. It was hit by a yellow car. IH8MOOVV was the last
car because it did not get hit from behind; this car hit the green car.

Questions About the Case

Set IV

1. What evidence can be gathered from the first vehicle? _____

_____

_____

_____

_____

_____

2. Predict who owns this vehicle. Give support for your answer. _____

_____

_____

_____

_____

_____

- -

Fold the following section under before copying this page for students.

Answers to Discussion Prompts (Set IV)

1. It has an opened pen and a pad of paper in the front seat. The radio was blasting static; the person was probably changing stations since people usually don't listen to static. The horn was soft. **2.** Answers will vary.

A PILE-UP OF CARS AND PROBLEMS

Questions About the Case

Set V

1. What evidence can be gathered from the second vehicle? _____

   _____

   _____

   _____

   _____

2. Predict who owns this vehicle. Give support for your answer. _____

   _____

   _____

   _____

   _____

3. Who was most likely driving behind this car? Why? _____

   _____

   _____

   _____

   _____

   _____

Fold the following section under before copying this page for students.

Answers to Discussion Prompts (Set V)

1. It has trees in the back. There was a sports talk program blasting on the radio. The steering was misaligned and the brakes needed to be adjusted. There is a newspaper in the front seat. **2.** The answer is Ken, because there are trees in the back. **3.** Anita was most likely behind this car, because she said she saw a nest in his car.

A PILE-UP OF CARS AND PROBLEMS

Questions About the Case

Set VI

1. What evidence can be gathered from the third vehicle? _____

_____

_____

_____

_____

_____

2. Predict who owns this vehicle. Give support for your answer. _____

_____

_____

_____

_____

_____

_____

Fold the following section under before copying this page for students.

Answers to Discussion Prompts (Set VI)

1. There is makeup in the front seat. There was a rock song playing loud on the radio. The driver would have to slam on the brakes for the car to stop.
2. Kelly probably owns this vehicle. She said she could not get a song out of her head, and rock music was playing in this vehicle.

A PILE-UP OF CARS AND PROBLEMS

Questions About the Case

Set VII

1. What evidence can be gathered from the fourth vehicle? _____

_____

_____

_____

_____

_____

2. Predict who owns this vehicle. Give support for your answer. _____

_____

_____

_____

_____

_____

_____

- -

Fold the following section under before copying this page for students.

Answers to Discussion Prompts (Set VII)

1. There are graded papers in the front seat. The brakes needed to be fixed. The radio was tuned to the news. **2.** The answer is most likely Otto, because there are graded papers on the passenger seat. Some students will say Anita. Have them look back at her statement: she says she needs to process overdue fines; a teacher would not do this, but a librarian would.

A PILE-UP OF CARS AND PROBLEMS

Mystery #7

N O   D E F E N S E

NOTE: All people in this story are fictional. (I bet you could have figured that out, though!)

Coach Ty Mout

NO DEFENSE

After losing the championship, Coach Ty Mout went to his office. He was not angry at his players: he was just in a state of disbelief. Two points was the difference between being champions for the third year in a row and losing their first game in years. How could his team, which has not lost a game in over three years, lose the biggest game of the year? He had five nationally-ranked starters who had full scholarships to the colleges of their choice for next year. The other team did not even have one nationally-ranked player. Besides the players' abilities, his team had beaten the other team on four separate occasions this season with an average point margin of 30.

The coach sat for hours replaying the game in his head and each time was left with only one conclusion: one of his players threw the game. He did not want to believe it, but the video replay and statistics from the game did not lie. He was now positive that one of his players did cheat and would have to be thrown off the team. He knew he had to be careful and absolutely certain because an accusation like this would affect a player's scholarship and future.

Coach Mout called each player into his office, looking for an answer. Each of the five starters denied knowing anything about throwing the game.

The Suspects

Luke Atmescore

Luke scored 34 points in the game. It was the most points of any player. People usually came to the games to see Luke's creative slam dunks. He had the crowd screaming with his four gravity-defying slam dunks. He did have a few embarrassing moments, though. The crowd screamed when he missed two layups. He tipped the ball into the opposing team's basket and scored for the other team on two separate occasions. He wanted to come out of the game at that point, but the coach needed his high-soaring scorer in the game. He also fell down twice while dribbling the ball, which resulted in steals and an easy four points for the other team. Luke made up for his mistakes with great defense. He blocked six shots without committing a single foul.

Trace Pointer

Trace scored the second-highest total points in the game, 20. He would have had more, but he was called for traveling and charging when he tried to make four layups. He did, however, have the most assists. In fact, he was one assist away from breaking the record. He will probably be remembered most for being the player who brought the ball up the court at the end of the game. As time was running out, he passed the ball with one second left on the clock. If the player would have made the shot, the team would have won and Trace would have broken the record: he also had the unfortunate event of being on the wrong side of a broken record. He had fouled Will Maketheshot on three occasions, who, in turn, broke the consecutive free-throws-made record of 88.

N O   D E F E N S E

The Suspects (cont.)

Al E. Oop

At first glance, Al's 15 points might not seem that impressive, but when you realize that his points were all scored in the first half of the game, it's amazing! As happy as the coach was for Al's offensive output, he was somewhat less than impressed because Al could play only half the game. Al and the player he was guarding had been going back and forth pushing and fouling each other during the first quarter. With two minutes left in the half, Al started fighting with the other player and was ejected from the game. His aggressive play earned him 15 points and a spot on the bench for the rest of the game.

Willy Everstopme

Willy is nothing short of a playmaker. People say he dribbles better than a leaky cup. He scored 10 points in the game, which is remarkable considering he had one of the league's top defenders guarding him the whole game. It is hard to tell if it was nerves or the defender's skills that caused Willy to throw the ball into the crowd five times. He also had the ball stolen three times. The last time, Willy got upset and received a technical for aggressively fouling the other player.

Phillip Thestands

Phillip scored the least amount of points: he only made three buckets, which resulted in six points. His scoring average is usually around 22 points per game. He also let the player he was guarding score eight easy baskets before asking the coach to be taken out of the game because his ankle hurt. Phillip rested on the bench with ice on his ankle until the last 15 seconds of the game. His team had possession of the ball and was going to take the last shot of the game. He was substituted back in and was the player to take the last shot. His half-court heave missed the basket completely.

NO DEFENSE

Questions About the Case

Set I

1. Can you formulate a theory for why a player would try to make his or her team lose? _____

_____

_____

_____

_____

_____

2. Why does Coach Ty Mout think one of his players threw the game?

_____

_____

_____

_____

_____

_____

- -

Fold the following section under before copying this page for students.

Answers to Discussion Prompts (Set I)

1. Answers will vary. **2.** The five players are five of the best in the country, and each made serious errors. The team had not lost for over three years. They had beaten the other team four times during the season by an average of 30 points.

NO DEFENSE

Questions About the Case

Set II

1. Looking at the aspects of a game of basketball (e.g., traveling, charging, assists, free throws), can you assess the importance of each element to prove which player is guilty of throwing the game? _____

   _____

   _____

   _____

   _____

2. Based on the evidence, how could you prove that Luke is innocent? How could you prove that he is guilty? _____

   _____

   _____

   _____

3. Do you think Trace threw the game? Why or why not? _____

   _____

   _____

   _____

   _____

Fold the following section under before copying this page for students.

Answers to Discussion Prompts (Set II)

1. Answers will vary. **2.** *To prove he's innocent:* He scored the most points. He blocked six shots. *To prove he's guilty:* He can slam dunk but missed two layups. He scored two baskets for the other team. He wanted to come out of the game. He fell down twice, which resulted in points for the other team. **3.** *To prove he's innocent:* He had the most assists. *To prove he's guilty:* Three times, he fouled a player who is known not to miss a shot. He scored 20 points but should have scored more. He charged and traveled. He had the ball the last 14 seconds of the game and passed it with only one second left.

NO DEFENSE

Questions About the Case

Set III

1. How could you determine if Al threw the game? _____

_____

_____

_____

2. Do you think Willy threw the game? Why or why not? _____

_____

_____

_____

3. What information would you use to support the view that Phillip is innocent? What information would you use to support the view that Phillip is guilty? _____

_____

_____

_____

N O   D E F E N S E

- -

Fold the following section under before copying this page for students.

Answers to Discussion Prompts (Set III)

1. One piece of evidence is particularly important: Al only played in the first half of the game. If a player was trying to throw the game, he would want to stay in the whole game so he could have more control over what happened.

2. *To prove he's innocent:* He scored 10 points against a good defender. *To prove he's guilty:* He threw the ball out of bounds five times. He had the ball stolen from him three times. He fouled a player because he was upset.

3. *To prove he's innocent:* He asked to be taken out of the game because his ankle hurt. *To prove he's guilty:* He scored 6 points; he usually scores 22. The player he was guarding scored eight times. He missed the last shot that would have won the game.

Mystery #1: Delivery or Take-out?

Clues Against Dee

☛ He has stolen before.

☛ His brother is a locksmith.

☛ He owes money.

☛ His fingerprints and footprints were found in the apartment.

☛ Two witnesses saw him.

Clues For Dee

☛ Both witnesses wear glasses.

☛ He could have been making a delivery when the doctor saw him.

☛ We do not know if his brother is close to Dee or lives by him.

☛ Shoplifting is different from breaking and entering.

☛ He could have saved the money to pay his bills and buy a computer.

☛ He has a credit card, which means he might be able to use it to purchase a computer.

☛ It does not say where the fingerprints were found.

☛ How would he know where Les kept the money?

Answer: This is a good mystery to start with since there is no definitive answer. All we know is that Les withdrew $10,000. We do not know what happened after that point.

Mystery #2:
The Canine Caper

Clues Against Herman

☛ He always loses to the Terriers; he is a sore loser.

☛ He was at the residence the day before the crime.

☛ He has unnecessary information in his note.

☛ He was heard making threats.

Clues Against Alice

☛ She has made threats before.

☛ She is the neighbor.

☛ She does not like animals.

Clues Against the Bulls

☛ Pete's medicine was filled the day after the crime.

☛ If Pete's reactions were so violent, his parents would make sure to have Pete stay away from animals. Therefore, he wouldn't need the allergy medicine.

☛ The footprints are running shoes. Alice's feet might be too small, and Herman might be too old to run.

☛ The ransom note reveals that the author knows the dog's name. The Bulls know Snowball's name because they have returned her to the Terriers before.

☛ The ransom note also reveals that the author knows the name of the Terriers' bank. The Bulls might know this because the Terriers could have paid for their dinner at the restaurant with a check.

Answer: The Bulls took Snowball.

Mystery #3:
A "Lotto" Lies

Clues Against Will

☛ He says he plays his daughters' birthdays, but the numbers cannot be birthdays since none of the months have 31 days. The months of the birthdays are February (2), April (4), and November (11). This leaves the days (18, 29, and 31). February, April, and November do not have 31 days, so the line that he always plays could only go up to 30.

☛ He checked carefully enough to realize two missing apples and a small amount of missing change, so he would have remembered to get his ticket back.

☛ The store was closed at the time the ticket was purchased.

☛ The ticket was actually purchased the day before Will asked Ivan to buy apples for him.

Clues Against Ivan

☛ Will dented his car and gave him a poor evaluation.

☛ Will got a promotion instead of Ivan.

☛ Ivan did not give back the change at first.

Answer: The ticket belongs to Ivan.

Mystery #4:
The Pupil with Peeking Pupils

Clues Against Paige

☞ She is a new student who might have trouble understanding the assignment.

☞ Stu is an honor-roll student.

☞ The teacher does not know Paige's writing.

Clues Against Stu

☞ They are both left-handed, but Stu is seated to Paige's right so it would be easier for him to see Paige's paper than it would be for Paige to see his.

☞ He always sat next to an honor-roll student, so he could have been copying all along.

☞ His paper does not have mistakes, because a person copying would most likely not copy mistakes.

☞ Paige is from Australia, which explains why the paper says "football" instead of "soccer."

☞ It would be warmer in Australia in December since it is located in the Southern Hemisphere. This explains why the person was able to wear shorts and play soccer.

Answer: Stu copied Paige's paper.

THE PUPIL WITH PEEKING PUPILS

Mystery #5: Running Home with a Home Run

Clues Against Owen

☛ He takes clients to games, but 8:30 on a Sunday night is not an ideal time for a business meeting.

☛ His ball has a grass stain, which could not have occurred in a domed stadium because there is no grass.

☛ He is a season-ticket holder, so he might park in the same place each game. That would explain why the parking spot might have been empty.

☛ The dent that he claims happened during the game is located at the bottom of his door. It's not likely that his car was dented by the other vehicles, since they are so high above the ground and his car is so low.

☛ He said he made a cell-phone call to his wife—so why did he then say he needed to race home to tell his wife the news?

☛ It never says where he made the call from.

Clues Against Jason

☛ The vendor could not recall Jason, and Jason did not have a receipt for the nachos.

☛ He purchased a ticket but may not have attended the game.

Answer: Jason A. Homer has the real baseball.

Mystery #6: A Pile-up of Cars and Problems

Clues Against Otto

- ☞ He was distracted by the person dancing; he might have been rehearsing his lecture.
- ☞ His brakes need to be fixed.
- ☞ He could have been grading papers.

Clues Against Ken

- ☞ He was angry about a player being traded.
- ☞ His radio was loud.
- ☞ He could have been reading the newspaper.
- ☞ He might have been driving too slowly because he did not want the trees to tip.
- ☞ His steering and brakes need to be fixed.

Clues Against Kelly

- ☞ She was listening to a loud song.
- ☞ She was dancing.
- ☞ She was in a hurry to get to the gym.
- ☞ She might have been putting on makeup.
- ☞ Her brakes needed to have extreme pressure applied to them.

Clues Against Anita

- ☞ She was the last car in the pile-up.
- ☞ She was the only one that was actually late.
- ☞ She was worried about getting written up at work.
- ☞ She was distracted by the trees in Ken's car.
- ☞ She must have been concentrating on the trees to spot a nest from her car.
- ☞ She was changing stations because the tuner was inbetween stations.
- ☞ Her radio was loud.

Answer: Anita caused the accident. The sequence of the accident pile-up: first—Kelly in the red car; second—Otto in the yellow car; third—Ken in the green car; fourth—Anita in the white car.

Mystery #7: No Defense

Clues Against Luke

☛ He can slam dunk but missed two layups.

☛ He scored for the other team.

☛ He fell down twice, which resulted in points for the other team.

Clues Against Trace

☛ His mistakes were not obvious mistakes. Someone that is cheating would not fall down or score for the other team because it would draw attention to him.

☛ He was in for the entire game: A player who is throwing the game would want to be involved so that he could make sure his team lost.

☛ Three times he fouled a player who would most likely make the free-throw shots.

☛ He had the ball for the last 14 seconds of the game and then passed the ball to a player standing at half court with only one second left. He could have passed it to someone sooner and closer to the basket.

Clues Against Al

☛ He was doing really well, so he got thrown out on purpose.

☛ He kept fouling so that the other team could get free throws.

Clues Against Willy

☛ If he were really good, he should have scored more than 10 points.

☛ He threw the ball into the stands five times.

☛ He had the ball stolen three times—a high number for someone known for his dribbling skills.

☛ He fouled the person and got a technical, which resulted in three free-throw shots.

Clues Against Phillip

☛ He scored a lot fewer points than normal.

☛ The person he was guarding scored 16 easy points.

☛ He went back into the game when it was on the line.

☛ He missed the last shot by a long shot.

Answer: Trace Pointer was the player who lost the game on purpose.

N O   D E F E N S E